Bre

igloo

igloo

Published by Igloo Books Ltd
Cottage Farm
Sywell
NN6 0BJ
www.igloo-books.com

10 9 8 7 6 5 4 3 2 1

ISBN: 978 1 84852 721 8

Project Managed by R&R Publications Marketing Pty Ltd

Food Photography: R&R Photostudio (www.rrphotostudio.com.au)
Recipe Development: R&R Test Kitchen

Front cover photograph © Stockfood/Oliver Brachat

Printed in and manufactured in China

Contents

Rich White Loaf

Preparation 20 mins **Cooking** 3 hrs **Calories** 2710

1 cup tepid water
1 large egg
1 tsp salt
1 tbsp sugar
3 tbsps butter or margarine
1 tbsp dough enhancer
600g (1¼lb) white bread flour
3 tsps instant dry yeast

1. Place all ingredients into the bread pan in the order listed, insert into the breadmaker and close the lid.
2. Program: Basic

   Size: Large

   Crust: Medium

Variation: Just before the baking cycle commences, open lid, brush top with milk and sprinkle with poppy seeds, if desired.

Soy and Linseed with Whole Wheat

Preparation 20 mins **Cooking** 3 hrs 40 mins **Calories** 1800

- 1¼ cups tepid water
- 1 tbsp olive oil
- 250g (9oz) soy and linseed bread mix
- 250g (9oz) whole wheat bread mix
- 2 tsps instant dry yeast

1. Place all ingredients into the bread pan in the order listed, insert into the breadmaker and close the lid.
2. Program: Wheat

   Size: Medium

   Crust: Medium

Herbed Cornbread

Preparation 20 mins **Cooking** 3 hrs **Calories** 2203

- 280ml (10 fl oz) tepid water
- 1 tbsp oil or margarine
- 1½ tbsps honey
- ½ tsp dried thyme
- 2 tbsps chopped fresh parsley
- 360g (12½oz) white bread mix
- 160g (5½oz) cornmeal flour or maize meal flour
- 1½ tsps instant dry yeast

1. Place all ingredients into the bread pan in the order listed, insert into the breadmaker and close the lid.
2. Program: Basic

   Size: Medium

   Crust: Light or Medium

Enriched Grain Bread

Preparation 25 mins **Cooking** 3 hrs **Calories** 1695

1 cup tepid water
2 tbsps brown sugar
2 tbsps margarine or butter
500g (18oz) grain bread mix
2 tsps instant dry yeast

1 Place all ingredients into the bread pan in the order listed, insert into the breadmaker and close the lid.

2 Program: Basic

Size: Large

Crust: Light or Medium

Note: Although the quantity of flour is not the usual quantity for a large loaf, choose Large Size as this loaf rises very high and also needs the extra cooking time.

Light Rye Bread

Light Rye Bread

Preparation 15 mins **Cooking** 3 hrs **Calories** 2672

- 350ml (12 fl oz) tepid water
- 1 tbsp margarine
- 1 tsp salt
- 2 tbsps honey
- 1 tbsp whole milk powder
- 1 tsp dough enhancer
- 450g (1lb) white bread flour
- 190g (7oz) rye flour
- 2 tsps instant dry yeast

1 Place all ingredients into the bread pan in the order listed, insert into the breadmaker and close the lid.

2 Program: Basic

Size: Medium

Crust: Dark

Special Whole Wheat Loaf

Preparation 15 mins **Cooking** 3 hrs 40 mins **Calories** 2625

- 310ml (10½ fl oz) tepid water
- 2 tbsps butter or margarine
- 1½ tbsps sugar
- 500g (18oz) whole wheat bread mix
- ½ cup instant potato flakes
- 2 tsps instant dry yeast

1 Place all ingredients into the bread pan in the order listed, insert into the breadmaker and close the lid.

2 Programs: Wheat

Size: Medium for standard, Large for larger

Crust: Medium

Diet Rye Loaf

Preparation 20 mins **Cooking** 3 hrs **Calories** 890

- 280ml (10 fl oz) tepid water
- ½ tsp salt
- ½ tsp sugar
- 1 tbsp skim milk powder
- 100g (4oz) white bread flour
- 150g (5oz) whole wheat flour
- 250g (9oz) rye flour
- 1 tbsp dough enhancer
- 1½ tsps instant dry yeast

1 Place all ingredients into the bread pan in the order listed, insert into the breadmaker and close the lid.

2 Program: Basic

Size: Medium

Crust: Medium

Note: Because the dough is dense, it tends to cook into a very uneven shape with a rough top. To avoid this, quickly remove the dough after the final knock down, knead the dough to reshape and place back in the bread pan.

Bran and Whole Wheat Loaf

Preparation 10 mins **Cooking** 3 hrs 40 mins **Calories** 2630

- 330ml (11 fl oz) tepid water
- 2 tbsps vegetable oil
- 2 tbsps honey
- 1 tsp salt
- ⅓ cup wheat bran
- 225g (9oz) whole wheat flour
- 300g (11oz) white bread flour
- 2 tsps instant dry yeast

1 Place all ingredients into the bread pan in the order listed, insert into the breadmaker and close the lid.

2 Program: Wheat

Size: Medium

Crust: Medium

High Fiber White Loaf with Oat Flour

Preparation 15 mins **Cooking** 3 hrs **Calories** 2598

- 400ml (14 fl oz) tepid water
- 1 tbsp whole milk powder
- ½ tsp salt
- 2 tsps margarine
- 500g (18oz) white bread mix
- 125g (4½oz) oat flour
- 3 tsps instant dry yeast

1. Place all ingredients into the bread pan in the order listed, insert into the breadmaker and close the lid.
2. Program: Basic

   Size: Medium

   Crust: Medium

Note: For an attractive topping, quickly open lid when baking cycle is about to commence, brush top of loaf with milk and sprinkle with oat flour. Oat flour may be found at health food stores, but it is very easy to make your own. Place rolled oats in a blender and process until finely ground – about 30 seconds.

Pumpernickle

Preparation 20 mins **Cooking** 3 hrs 40 mins **Calories** 2562

- 260ml (9 fl oz) tepid water
- 2 tbsps vegetable oil
- 2 tbsps molasses
- 2 tbsps brown sugar
- 1½ tsps instant coffee granules
- 2 tsps caraway seeds
- 125g (4½oz) rye meal flour
- 125g (4½oz) whole wheat flour
- 300g (11oz) white bread flour
- 1½ tsps instant dry yeast

1 Place all ingredients into the bread pan in the order listed, insert into the breadmaker and close the lid.

2 Program: Wheat

Size: Medium

Crust: Medium

Note: Because this is a very heavy dough, it tends to bake in an uneven shape. To avoid this, quickly remove the dough after the final knock down, knead the dough to reshape and place back in the bread pan.

Tomato and Basil Bread

Preparation 10 mins **Cooking** 3 hrs **Calories** 2128

300ml (10 fl oz) tepid water
1 tbsp olive oil
1 tbsp grated onion
2 tbsps chopped fresh basil or 1 tsp dried basil
1½ tbsps tomato paste
2 tsps sugar
500g (18oz) white bread mix
2 tsps instant dry yeast

1 Place ingredients into the bread pan in the order listed, insert into the breadmaker and close the lid.

2 Program: Basic

Size: Medium

Crust: Medium

Salami and Cheese Loaf

Preparation 20 mins **Cooking** 3 hrs **Calories** 2200

300ml (10 fl oz) water
½ tsp dried oregano
50g (2oz) salami, coarsely chopped
50g (2oz) sharp cheddar cheese, grated
500g (18oz) white bread mix
2 tsps instant dry yeast

1 Place ingredients into the bread pan in the order listed, insert into the breadmaker and close the lid.

2 Program: Basic

Size: Medium

Crust: Medium

Note: The kneading process of the breadmaker breaks up the salami, making it less visible in the bread. For more obvious chunks of salami, chop it very coarsely. For an interesting topping, 20 minutes before completion of the baking cycle sprinkle top with extra grated cheddar cheese.

Top: Tomato and Basil Bread
Bottom: Toasted Salami and Cheese Loaf

Sweet Potato and Grain Loaf

Sweet Potato and Grain Loaf

Preparation 10 mins **Cooking** 3 hrs **Calories** 2108

- 1 cup tepid water
- 1 egg
- 1 tbsp margarine or butter
- 1½ tbsps brown sugar
- ¾ cup cooked mashed sweet potato
- 500g (18oz) grain bread mix
- 1 tsp ground ginger
- 2 tsps instant dry yeast

1 Place ingredients into the bread pan in the order listed, insert into the breadmaker and close the lid.

2 Program: Basic

Size: Medium

Crust: Medium

Note: Use the water from the boiled sweet potato to make the bread. Cool to tepid before adding.

Zucchini, Soy and Linseed Loaf

Preparation 10 mins **Cooking** 3 hrs **Calories** 2000

1 cup tepid water
1 tbsp oil
1 tbsp honey
¾ cup sliced zucchini (2 medium)
500g (18oz) soy and linseed bread mix
2 tsps instant dry yeast

1. Place ingredients into the bread pan in the order listed, insert into the breadmaker and close the lid.
2. Program: Basic

   Size: Medium

   Crust: Medium

Mushroom, Soy and Linseed Loaf

Preparation 25 mins **Cooking** 3 hrs **Calories** 2221

2 tbsps olive oil
1 medium onion, finely chopped.
150g (5oz) mushrooms, thinly sliced.
230ml (8 fl oz) tepid water
2 tbsps lemon juice
1 quantity onion and mushroom mixture (above)
500g (18oz) soy and linseed bread mix
2 tsps instant dry yeast

1. Heat oil in pan. Add onions and cook for 3 minutes. Add mushrooms, cook until soft. Allow to cool completely.
2. Place ingredients into the bread pan in the order listed, insert into the breadmaker and close the lid.
3. Program: Basic

   Size: Medium

   Crust: Medium

Gherkin and Sweet Corn

Preparation 10 mins **Cooking** 3 hrs **Calories** 2046

250ml (8½ fl oz) tepid water
1 egg
1 tbsp margarine
125g (5oz) can sweet corn
500g (18oz) white bread mix
½ cup chopped gherkins
2 tsps instant dry yeast

1. Place ingredients into the bread pan in the order listed, insert into the breadmaker and close the lid.
2. Program: White

   Size: Large

   Crust: Medium

Pesto and Pine Nut Loaf

Preparation 15 mins **Cooking** 3 hrs **Calories** 2527

300ml (10 fl oz) tepid water
1 tbsp olive oil
1½ tsps crushed garlic
½ cup fresh basil leaves
3 tbsps grated parmesan cheese
500g (18oz) white bread mix
2 tsps instant dry yeast

In Auto Fruit and Nut Dispenser
3 tbsps pine nuts

1. Place ingredients into the bread pan in the order listed, insert into the breadmaker and close the lid.
2. Place pine nuts in the Automatic Fruit and Nut Dispenser.
3. Program: Basic

   Size: Medium

   Crust: Medium

Sun-dried Tomato Loaf

Preparation 15 mins **Cooking** 3 hrs **Calories** 2326

300ml (10 fl oz) tepid water
1 tbsp oil, from sun-dried tomatoes
2 tsps sugar
500g (18oz) white bread mix
4 tbsps sun-dried tomatoes, drained from oil
2 tsps instant dry yeast

1. Place ingredients into the bread pan in the order listed, insert into the breadmaker and close the lid.
2. Program: Basic

   Size: Medium

   Crust: Medium

Quick Pesto Loaf

Preparation 20 mins **Cooking** 3 hrs **Calories** 2245

290ml (10 fl oz) tepid water
1 tbsp olive oil
2½ tbsps bottled pesto sauce
500g (18oz) white bread mix
2 tsps instant dry yeast

1. Place ingredients into the bread pan in the order listed, insert into the breadmaker and close the lid.
2. Program: Basic

   Size: Medium

   Crust: Medium

Left: Sun-dried Tomato Loaf
Right: Pesto and Pinenut Loaf

Carrot and Golden Raisin Grain Loaf

Preparation 10 mins **Cooking** 3 hrs **Calories** 2511

- 1 cup tepid water
- 1 tbsp butter or margarine
- 1½ tbsps brown sugar
- 2 cups shredded carrot
- 500g (18oz) grain bread mix
- ½ cup golden raisins
- 1 tsp cinnamon
- 2 tsps instant dry yeast

1. Place ingredients into the bread pan in the order listed, insert into the breadmaker and close the lid.
2. Program: Basic

   Size: Medium

   Crust: Medium

Onion, Soy and Linseed Loaf

Preparation 20 mins **Cooking** 3 hrs **Calories** 2042

- 1 large onion, chopped
- 1 tbsp vegetable oil
- 1 cup water
- 1½ tsps curry powder
- 500g (18oz) soy and linseed bread mix
- 2 tsps instant dry yeast

1 Cook the onion in the oil until soft and golden.

2 Place ingredients into the bread pan in the order listed, insert into the breadmaker and close the lid.

3 Program: Basic

Size: Medium

Crust: Medium

Peanut Butter and Sesame Loaf

Preparation 10 mins **Cooking** 3 hrs 40 mins **Calories** 2760

- 300ml (10 fl oz) tepid water
- 2 tbsps honey
- ⅓ cup peanut butter
- 500g (18oz) whole wheat bread mix
- 2 tbsps sesame seeds
- 2 tsps instant dry yeast

1 Place ingredients into the bread pan in the order listed, insert into the breadmaker and close the lid.

2 Program: Wheat

Size: Medium

Crust: Medium

Orange and Poppy Seed Bread

Preparation 10 mins **Cooking** 3 hrs **Calories** 2305

- zest of 2 oranges
- Juice of 2 oranges, plus enough water to measure 300ml (10 fl oz)
- 1 tbsp butter
- 1 tbsp honey
- 500g (18oz) whole wheat bread mix
- 40g (1½oz) poppy seeds
- 2 tsps instant dry yeast

1 Place ingredients into the bread pan in the order listed, insert into the breadmaker and close the lid.

2 Program: Basic

Size: Medium

Crust: Medium

Orange and Poppy Seed Bread

Feta Cheese and Olive Bread

Preparation 15 mins **Cooking** 3 hrs **Calories** 2197

280ml (10 fl oz) tepid water

125g (4½oz) Feta cheese, crumbled

1 tbsp chopped fresh parsley or rosemary

500g (18oz) whole wheat bread mix

2 tsps instant dry yeast

In Auto Fruit and Nut Dispenser

3 tbsps black olives, sliced

1. Place ingredients into the bread pan in the lorder listed, insert into the breadmaker and close the lid.
2. Add olives to the Automatic Fruit and Nut Dispenser
3. Program: White

   Size: Large

   Crust: Medium

Note: If your breadmaker does not have a dispenser, add the olives towards the end of the kneading process. The moisture content of the Feta cheese will vary. Check the dough about 8 minutes into mixing. If it is too dry, add more water or if too moist, add more flour.

Garlic Bread

Preparation 10 mins **Cooking** 3 hrs **Calories** 2691

280ml (10 fl oz) tepid water
1 tsp salt
2 tsps sugar
3 tbsps butter or margarine
2 tsps chopped fresh garlic or more to taste
600g (1⅓ lb) white bread flour
2 tsps instant dry yeast

1 Place ingredients into the bread pan in the order listed, insert into the breadmaker andclose the lid.

2 Program: White

Size: Large

Crust: Medium

Roasted Pumpkin Bread

Preparation 20 mins **Cooking** 3 hrs **Calories** 2067

310ml (10½ fl oz) tepid water
¾ cup roasted pumpkin
1½ tsps nutmeg
½ tsp cinnamon
1 tbsp brown sugar
500g (18oz) white bread mix
2 tsps instant dry yeast

1 Place ingredients into the bread pan in the order listed, insert into the breadmaker and close the lid.

2 Program: White

Size: Large

Crust: Medium

Pea and Bacon Loaf

Preparation 30 mins **Cooking** 3 hrs **Calories** 2984

Pre-preparation
1½ cups frozen peas
1½ cups boiling water
½ tsp salt
1 tsp sugar
4 slices bacon, chopped
1 cup cooking liquid and water
1 egg
pre-prepared peas
pre-prepared bacon
1 tbsp bacon fat from the pan.
600g (1⅓ lb) white bread flour
1 tbsp dough enhancer
3 tsps instant dry yeast

1 Cook the peas in the boiling salted water with sugar added. Drain and reserve the cooking water. Measure the cooking water and add enough cold water to bring to 250ml (8½ fl oz). Cool peas completely.

2 Trim rind and some of the fat from the bacon and cook in a heated pan until the bacon is cooked but not crisp. Reserve cooking fat. Allow bacon and fat to cool.

3 Place ingredients into the bread pan in the order listed, insert into the breadmaker and close the lid.

4 Program: White

Size: Large

Crust: Medium

Left: Roasted Pumpkin Bread
Right: Pea and Bacon Loaf

Raisin and Walnut Whole Wheat

Preparation 15 mins **Cooking** 3 hrs 40 mins **Calories** 2847

300ml (10 fl oz) tepid water
1 tbsp margarine
1½ tbsps brown sugar
500g (18oz) whole wheat bread mix
2 tsps instant dry yeast

In Auto Fruit and Nut Dispenser
½ cup raisins
¼ cup chopped walnuts

1 Place ingredients into the bread pan in the order listed, insert into the breadmaker and close lid.

2 Add raisins and walnuts to the Automatic Fruit and Nut Dispenser

3 Program: Wheat

Size: Medium

Crust: Medium

Note: If your machine does not have a dispenser, add the raisins and walnuts after the fruit and nut beeper indicates when to add.

Date and Pecan Whole Wheat

Preparation 10 mins **Cooking** 3 hrs 40 mins **Calories** 2622

300ml (10 fl oz) tepid water
2 tbsps brown sugar or honey
1 tbsp margarine
500g (18oz) whole wheat bread mix
2 tsps instant dry yeast

In Auto Fruit and Nut Dispenser
½ cup chopped dates
½ cup coarsely chopped pecan nuts

1 Place ingredients into the bread pan in the order listed, insert into the breadmaker and close the lid.

2 Add dates and pecans to the Automatic Fruit and Nut Dispensor.

3 Program: Wheat

Size: Large

Crust: Medium

Note: If your machine does not have a dispenser, add the dates and pecan nuts after the fruit and nut beeper indicates when to add.

Left: Date and Pecan Whole Wheat
Right: Raisin and Walnut Whole Wheat

Brioche Loaf

Preparation 10 mins **Cooking** 2 hrs 50 mins **Calories** 2649

- 150ml (5 fl oz) tepid water
- 2 tbsps sugar
- 90g (3oz) sweet butter, at room temperature
- 2 tsps lemon juice
- 2 eggs
- 500g (18oz) white bread mix
- 2 tsps instant dry yeast

1. Place ingredients into the bread pan in the order listed, insert into the breadmaker and close the lid.
2. Program: Sweet

   Size: Large

   Crust: Medium

Mango and Orange Spiced Bread

Preparation 10 mins **Cooking** 2 hrs 50 mins **Calories** 2321

- 300ml (10 fl oz) fresh orange juice and water (tepid)
- zest of 2 oranges
- 3 tbsps caster sugar
- 1 tbsp butter or margarine
- 500g (18oz) white bread mix
- 1 tbsp dough enhancer
- ½ tsp cinnamon
- ¼ tsp nutmeg
- ¼ tsp vanilla sugar
- 65g (2½oz) dried mango, chopped
- 2 tsps instant dry yeast

1. Zest the oranges first, then juice them and add enough water to come to 300ml (10 fl oz).
2. Place ingredients into the bread pan in the order listed, insert into the breadmaker and close the lid.
3. Program: Sweet

   Size: Medium

   Crust: Medium

Golden Raisin Honey Loaf

Preparation 12 mins **Cooking** 2 hrs 50 mins **Calories** 2545

280ml (10 fl oz) tepid water
2½ tbsps honey
1 tsp cinnamon
500g (18oz) white bread mix
2 tsps instant dry yeast

In Auto Fruit and Nut Dispenser
½ to ¾ cup golden raisins

1. Place ingredients into the bread pan in the order listed, insert into the breadmaker and close the lid.
2. Add golden raisins to the Automatic Fruit and Nut Dispenser
3. Program: Sweet

   Size: Medium

   Crust: Medium

Chocolate Bread

Preparation 10 mins **Cooking** 2 hrs 50 mins **Calories** 2870

320ml (11 fl oz) tepid water
1 tbsp margarine
1½ tbsps cocoa powder
½ cup chocolate chips
3 tbsps sugar
500g (18oz) white bread mix
2 tsps instant dry yeast

1 Place ingredients into the bread pan in the order listed, insert into the breadmaker and close the lid.

2 Program: Sweet

Size: Medium

Crust: Light

Rum and Hazelnut Chocolate Chip

Preparation 10 mins **Cooking** 2 hrs 50 mins **Calories** 4043

280ml (10 fl oz) water
4 tbsps sugar
500g (18oz) white bread mix
1 cup ground hazelnuts
2 tsps rum extract
1 tsp bread improver
2 tsps instant dry yeast
1 cup chocolate chips

1 Place ingredients into the bread pan in the order listed, insert into the breadmaker and close the lid.

2 Program: Sweet

Size: Medium

Crust: Medium

Cherry Party Bread

Preparation 15 mins **Cooking** 2 hrs 50 mins **Calories** 2585

290ml (10 fl oz) water
1 tbsp margarine
2 tbsps sugar
½ tsp vanilla sugar
500g (18oz) white bread mix
2 tsps instant dry yeast

In Auto Fruit and Nut Dispenser
200g (7oz) candied cherries, halved

1 Place ingredients into the bread pan in the order listed, insert into the breadmaker and close the lid.

2 Add cherries to the Automatic Fruit and Nut Dispenser.

3 Program: White

Size: Large

Crust: Light

Note: If your machine does not have a dispenser, add the cherries after the fruit and nut beeper indicates when to add.

Golden Lemon Nuggets

Preparation 50 mins **Cooking** 1 hr **Calories** 2573

160ml (5½ fl oz) tepid water
1 tbsp butter
1 tbsp lemon juice
½ tsp salt
3 tbsps superfine sugar
300g (11oz) white bread flour
½ tsp vanilla sugar
1½ tsps instant dry yeast

Lemon Glaze

3 tbsps superfine sugar
grated zest of 1 lemon
2 tsps lemon juice
1 tbsp melted butter

1 Mix ingredients until combined.

2 Place ingredients into the bread pan in the order listed, insert into the breadmaker and close the lid. Select the Dough setting and press Start.

3 When dough is ready, remove to a floured board, pat out to a rectangle and cut into 16 to 20 small squares.

4 Take a piece of cooking parchment and mold around the kneading blade in the breadpan. Then place a double thickness of cooking parchment into the bread pan to line the base and to come over the tip of the kneading blade and a little way up the sides.

5 Dip each square into the lemon glaze to coat all sides, and arrange in the bread pan, around the sides first then over the blade.

6 Place pan back into the machine and press Bake. After 5 minutes press Pause or Stop, this will give enough heat for rising. Allow to rise for 30 minutes then restart the machine by pressing the Start button to continue the cycle or re-program bake and press Start.

7 Brush top 2 or 3 times during the last half of the cooking time with lemon glaze to give a golden crust. Nuggets may be ready 10 minutes before end of program time, remove from machine if cooked and a good color.

Note: If your breadmaker does not have a Bake option, place nuggets on a lined baking tray and bake in your oven at180°C (350°F) for 30 minutes.

Panettone

Preparation 25 mins **Cooking** 2 hr 50 mins **Calories** 2980

- 150ml (5 fl oz) tepid water
- ½ tsp salt
- 1 tbsp whole milk powder
- 3 tbsps superfine sugar
- 2 x 60g (2oz) eggs
- 2 x 60g (2oz) egg yolks
- 80g (3oz) sweet butter, softened
- zest of 1 orange
- zest of 1 lemon
- 1 tbsp lemon juice
- 500g (18oz) white bread flour
- 2 tsps instant dry yeast

In Auto Fruit and Nut Dispenser

- 2 tbsps mixed peel
- ½ cup raisins

1. Stand butter and eggs at room temperature for 1 hour before mixing the bread.
2. Place ingredients into the bread pan in the order listed, insert into the breadmaker and close the lid.
3. Add mixed peel and raisins to the Automatic Fruit and Nut Dispenser
4. Program: Sweet

   Size: Large

   Crust: Medium

Note: If your machine does not have a dispenser, add the mixed peel and raisins after the fruit and nut beeper indicates when to add.

Spiced Fruit Loaf

Preparation 15 mins **Cooking** 2 hrs 50 mins **Calories** 2513

280ml (10 fl oz) tepid water
1 tbsp butter
2 tbsps sugar
1 tsp cinnamon
⅛ tsp ground cloves
500g (18oz) white bread mix
2 tsps instant dry yeast

In Auto Fruit and Nut Dispenser
150g (5oz) mixed dried fruit

1. Place ingredients into the bread pan in the order listed, insert into the breadmaker and close the lid.
2. Add fruit mix to the Automatic Fruit and Nut Dispenser.
3. Program: Sweet

   Size: Large

   Crust: Medium

Vegetable Pouches

Preparation 35 mins **Cooking** 1 hr 30 mins **Calories** 1887

Bread Dough

160ml (5½ fl oz) tepid water

½ tsp salt

1 tbsp margarine or oil

300g (11oz) white bread flour

1 tsp instant dry yeast

1 beaten egg and water for glazing

poppy seeds or other garnish, optional

Vegetable Filling

400g (14oz) pumpkin or sweet potato boiled and mashed

6 shallots, finely chopped

¾ cup frozen baby peas, cooked and drained

100g (4oz) tasty cheddar cheese, grated

½ tsp nutmeg

salt and pepper to taste

2 eggs, beaten

1 To make the Bread Dough: place all ingredients into the bread pan in the order listed, insert into the breadmaker and close the lid.

2 Program: Dough, Press: Start.

3 Meanwhile prepare the filling (see below).

4 To make the Vegetable Filling: Combine all ingredients for filling.

5 Turn the completed dough onto a lightly floured surface. Roll out the dough to a 4mm (⅕in) thickness. Cut into rounds approximately 13cm (5in) in diameter.

6 Place about 2 tbsps of filling into the center. Lift the dough up the side of the filling and press together to form a pouch. Open the frill on top a little. Brush with egg glaze and sprinkle with poppy, caraway or sunflower seeds, if desired. Repeat with remainder.

7 Place in preheated oven (200°C/400°F) and cook for 15 to 20 minutes. Serve hot or cold with a salad garnish.

Variation: Garlic mashed potato with peas, Parmesan, parsley and fried onion.

Bacon Turnovers

Preparation 35 mins **Cooking** 1 hr 30 mins **Calories** 3600

Bread Dough

1 cup water

1 tbsp whole milk powder

120g (4oz) butter, melted and cooled

2 tbsps sugar

1 egg yolk

500g (18oz) white bread mix

2 tsps instant dry yeast

Filling

2 tbsps oil

1 onion, diced

250g (9oz) bacon, finely chopped

1 tsp white pepper

1 Place all ingredients into the bread pan in the order listed, insert into the breadmaker and close the lid. Program: Dough, Press: Start.

2 Meanwhile prepare the filling (see below).

3 Heat the oil in a pan, add onions, and stir to fry a little. Cover with a lid, reduce heat to low and allow to cook for 2 minutes, stirring occasionally until soft and golden. Remove and place in a bowl.

4 Add chopped bacon to the pan and fry lightly until cooked but not crisp. Drain off any fat, mix into the onions with the white pepper. Set aside to cool completely.

5 When dough is ready turn out onto a lightly floured board and leave it as is.

6 Pull out an edge of the dough and flatten into a round shape with your fist. Place about 1 tsp of filling 2cm (¾in) in from the edge, brush edge with water and fold dough over filling.

7 Cut away with a 6cm (2¼in) cutter or glass, to resemble a half moon. Repeat until all dough and filling is used.

8 Place seam side down on a greased baking tray, cover and set in a warm place to rise for 15 minutes. Brush with egg and milk glaze and bake in a hot oven (220°C/425°F) for 5 to 7 minutes. Serve hot.

9 Larger Size – Roll out dough and cut into rounds with a 9cm or 12cm (3½ or 4¾in) cutter. Place filling on one half, wet edges and fold other half over and seal. Bake in an oven at 200°C (400°F) for 10 to 15 minutes.

Salmon Pie

Preparation 40 mins **Cooking** 1 hr 30 mins **Calories** 3166

Bread Dough
- 120ml (4 fl oz) tepid water
- ½ tsp salt
- 2 tsps sugar
- 1 egg yolk
- 60g (2oz) butter, softened
- 350g (12oz) white bread flour
- 1½ tsps instant dry yeast

Filling
- 415g (14oz) can red salmon
- 2 tbsps oil
- 1 large onion, finely chopped
- 125g (4½oz) mushrooms, sliced
- 1 cup cooked rice
- 1 tbsp chopped fresh dill
- 2 hard cooked eggs, chopped
- 2 tbsps lemon juice
- salt and pepper to taste

1. Place all ingredients into the bread pan in the order listed, insert into breadmaker and close the lid.
2. Program: Dough Press: Start.
3. Meanwhile prepare the filling (see below).Drain salmon and remove skin, flake with a fork.
4. Heat oil in a pan, sauté onion until soft, add mushrooms and cook a little.
5. In a bowl mix the salmon with the onion and mushrooms, and remaining ingredients.
6. When the dough is ready, turn out onto a lightly floured board and roll into a rectangle shape 25cm x 30cm (10 x 12in).
7. Pile the filling in a 7cm (2½in) wide strip along the centre of the longer side and 1½ cm (½in) from each end. Close the pie by bringing up the dough on each side of filling to meet edge to edge. Fold edge over and crimp with fingers to seal. Place onto a greased baking tray. Stand covered for 10 minutes to prove a little.
8. Brush top with milk and place in a preheated oven at 200°C (400°F) for 30–35 minutes. Serve hot or cold with a salad.

Pesto Roulade

Preparation 40 mins **Cooking** 1 hr 30 mins **Calories** 4080

- 1 cup tepid water
- 2 tbsps olive oil
- ¼ tsp salt
- 1 tsp sugar
- 400g (14oz) white bread flour
- 1½ tsps instant dry yeast

Filling

- 200g (7oz) cheddar cheese cut into wide fingers
- 200g (7oz) jar pesto sauce or ¾ cup homemade pesto
- 100g (4oz) toasted pine nuts
- poppy seeds for topping

1. Place all ingredients into the bread pan in the order listed, insert into the breadmaker and close the lid.
2. Program: Dough Press: Start.
3. Turn completed dough onto a lightly floured surface. Roll to a rectangular shape 1½cm (½in) thick and approximately 28 x 35cm (11 x 14in).
4. Place a line of cheese fingers across the narrow edge of the dough and 4cm (1½in) in from the edge. Spoon a row of pesto 3cm (1in) from and parallel to the cheese. Repeat with 3 more rows of cheese and pesto, spacing 3cm (1in) apart. Sprinkle the pine nuts all over the surface.
5. Fold the edge of the dough over the first row of cheese and pesto, and continue to roll over each pair of cheese and pesto rows. Sprinkle the work surface with poppy seeds and roll the roulade over them to press them into the dough.
6. Place seam side down on a greased baking tray, cover with a clean towel and allow to rise for 40 minutes. Bake in a preheated oven at 180°C (350°F) for 30 minutes until golden. Remove to a wire rack to cool. Serve warm, cut into thick slices. It is great to serve as finger food with drinks and to accompany salad meals.

Bread-Crusted Meat Pies

Preparation 45 mins **Cooking** 1 hr 30 mins **Calories** 303

Bread Cases

260ml (9 fl oz) tepid water

2 tbsps olive oil

1 tbsp lemon juice

1 tsp sugar

½ clove garlic, crushed

1 tsp salt

400g (14 oz) white bread flour

1½ tsps instant dry yeast

Meat Filling

2 tbsps olive oil

1 large onion, finely chopped

1 clove garlic, crushed

400g (14oz) ground beef

½ cup chopped tomatoes in juice (from can)

2 tsps tomato paste

½ cup water

salt, pepper to season

1 tbsp chopped parsley

1 tsp dried mixed herbs

2 tbsps grated Parmesan cheese

1 egg

poppy or sesame seeds for topping

1 Place bread ingredients into the bread pan in the order listed, insert into the breadmaker and close the lid.

2 Program: Dough Press: Start.

3 Meanwhile prepare the filling. Heat the oil in a skillet, add onion and garlic and cook until golden. Add mince and stir to brown throughout, breaking up any lumps.

4 Add tomato, tomato paste, water, seasonings, parsley and herbs. Cover and simmer for 25 minutes. Uncover and continue to cook until most of the liquid has been absorbed.

5 Transfer to a bowl and cool well. Stir in the Parmesan cheese and egg.

6 When dough is ready, turn out onto a floured board. Divide in 2. Roll each half out to ½ cm (⅕in) thickness. Cut out 12 rounds with 10cm (4in) cutter and 12 rounds with a 6cm or 7cm (2¼ or 2½in) cutter.

7 Grease a 12 hole muffin pan (medium size). Insert the larger rounds into the muffin cups, moulding the dough into the side. Fill with 1½ tbsps of beef filling, packing down well.Wet the dough rim with water and place the smaller rounds on the top. Press around edge to seal. Brush with milk and sprinkle with poppy or sesame seeds.

8 Bake at 200°C (400°F) for 20–25 minutes or until golden brown. Serve hot with steamed vegetables and brown gravy or hot tomato salsa.

Note: These pies may be frozen and reheated.

Herb Focaccia Rounds

Preparation 40 mins **Cooking** 1 hr 30 mins **Calories** 1765

- 260ml (9 fl oz) tepid water
- 2 tbsps olive oil
- 1 ½ tsps salt
- ½ tsp sugar
- 400g (14oz) white bread flour
- 1 tsp instant dry yeast
- ½ tsp dried rosemary
- fresh sprig of rosemary
- sea salt to garnish

1 Place all ingredients into the bread pan in the order listed, insert into the breadmaker and close the lid.

2 Program: Dough Press: Start.

3 Turn the completed dough out onto a lightly floured board. Divide into 3. Roll each portion into a circle about 1cm (⅓in) thick. Place onto greased baking trays, cover with a towel and stand in a warm place to rise for 30 to 40 minutes.

4 Make deep dents over the surface with fingertips, brush with oil. Place a small sprig of fresh rosemary into some of the dents.

5 Place in a preheated oven, 180°C (350°F) for 15–20 minutes or until golden.

Calzone Loaf

Preparation 45 mins **Cooking** 1 hr 30 mins **Calories** 3835

Bread Dough
- 1 cup tepid water
- ¼ cup olive oil
- 1 tsp sugar
- ¼ tsp salt
- 400g (14oz) white bread flour
- 1½ tsps instant dry yeast

Filling
- 3 tbsps olive oil
- 1 medium red onion, chopped
- 1 clove garlic, crushed
- 1 red pepper seeded and chopped
- 1 medium eggplant, diced
- 250g (9oz) Feta cheese, diced
- 100g (2oz) grated Parmesan cheese
- 1 tbsp chopped fresh parsley
- 1 tsp dried thyme or sage
- salt and pepper to taste
- egg and water for brushing
- 1 tbsp toasted sesame seeds

1 To make the Bread Dough: place ingredients into the bread pan in the order listed, insert into the breadmaker and close the lid.

2 Program: Dough Press: Start.

3 Meanwhile prepare the filling (see below).

4 To make the Filling: heat the olive oil in a saucepan; add the onion, garlic, pepper and eggplant. Stir and fry a little. Place lid on saucepan, allow to simmer for 10 minutes stirring occasionally. Remove from heat and allow to cool. Add the cheeses, parsley and seasonings.

5 Turn completed dough onto a lightly floured surface, punch down then roll out to a rectangle, 26cm by 38cm (10 x 15in).

6 With the longer side in front of you (parallel to bench edge) spread the filling across the centre in a 7cm (2½in) wide strip and 2cm (¾in) in from each end. Wet the edges of the dough with egg glaze. Lift both sides of the dough over the filling to meet edge to edge in the center. Press ends to seal and then tuck ends underneath. Place on a greased baking tray, cover and stand in a warm place to rise for 20 minutes.

7 Brush well with egg wash and sprinkle with sesame seeds. Bake in a pre-heated oven at 200°C (400°F) for 30 minutes or until golden and cooked.

Herbed Pizza Base

Preparation 30 mins **Cooking** 1 hr 30 mins **Calories** 1392

- ½ cup tepid water
- 1 tbsp olive oil
- ½ tsp salt
- ½ tsp sugar
- ½ clove garlic, crushed
- ½ tsp dried oregano
- 2 tbsps chopped fresh parsley
- 250g (8½oz) white bread flour
- 1 tsp instant dry yeast
- 2 tbsps extra virgin olive oil
- 1 red chili, seeded and finely chopped
- 1 clove garlic, finely chopped

1. Place all ingredients into the bread pan in the order listed, insert into the breadmaker and close the lid.
2. Program: Pizza Dough or Dough Press: Start.
3. Divide completed dough into three. Roll each into a round approximately 14cm (5in) diameter. Place onto greased baking trays, cover and stand for 10 minutes to rise.
4. Brush with extra virgin olive oil and sprinkle with red chili and garlic. Bake in a preheated oven at 250°C (480°F) for 5 to 10 minutes.
5. When cooked, place on plate and top with salad greens and marinated roasted vegetables, such as eggplant, semi-dried tomatoes and zucchini.

Salad with Mini Rolls or Croutons

Preparation 35 mins **Cooking** 1 hr 30 mins **Calories** 1410

210ml (7½ fl oz) tepid water
1 tbsp margarine
1 tbsp lemon juice
1 x 60g (2oz) egg
½ tsp crushed garlic
350g (12oz) white bread flour
1½ tsps instant dry yeast

1. Place ingredients into the bread pan in the order listed, insert into the breadmaker and close the lid.
2. Program: Dough Press: Start.
3. Turn completed dough onto a lightly floured surface. Break off pieces and form into tiny balls ½ cm (⅕in) in diameter; roll some dough into thin straws and form into mini twists and scrolls. Roll out remaining dough and cut into tiny cubes. Place all onto greased baking trays. Cover and allow to rise for 10 minutes.
4. Brush with milk and bake in moderate oven 180°C (350°F) for 10 to 15 minutes. Cool well and store in an airtight container or freeze.
5. Prepare a salad of choice. Toss in the mini rolls.

Note: Make a batch of bread croûtons and store in the freezer. Use to add to salads, soups and stews. They are a healthier alternative to fried croutons.

Pocket Bread

Preparation 30 mins **Cooking** 1 hr 30 mins **Calories** 1766g

1 cup tepid water
2 tbsps olive oil
1 tsp sugar
½ tsp salt
400g (14oz) white bread flour
1 tsp instant dry yeast

1 Place all ingredients into the bread pan in the order listed, insert into breadmaker and close the lid.

2 Program: Dough Press: Start.

3 Remove completed dough to a floured board and divide into 12 portions. Take one portion and roll out to a 12–13cm (4½–5in) circle. Make a cut from the center to the outside edge. Pick up the cut edge and roll all the way around the circle, rolling into a cone shape, trapping in air that will form the pocket. Stand cone on its point and press the top down to form a ball again. Roll out into a 12cm (4½in) circle; roll on one side only. Place on a towel and cover while the remainders are rolled. Allow to rise for 10 to 15 minutes.

4 Preheat oven 220°C (425°F) and heat the baking trays. Quickly remove a hot tray; spray lightly with an oil spray and place on the 3 breads. Quickly place back in the oven and cook until puffed and golden, about 4 to 6 minutes. Cook remainder.

5 Serve, filled with salad ingredients, hummus or yogurt sauce and slices of chicken or other meats.

Hamburger Bun

Preparation 40 mins **Cooking** 1 hr **Calories** 1936

- 280ml (10 fl oz) tepid water
- 1 tbsp margarine
- 1 x 60g (2oz) egg
- 500g (18oz) white bread mix
- 1½ tsps instant dry yeast
- 1 tsp sesame seeds

1. Place all ingredients into the bread pan in the order listed, insert into the breadmaker and close the lid.
2. Program: Dough Press: Start.
3. Turn completed dough onto a lightly floured surface. Divide into 6 equal pieces then roll each piece into a 13cm (5in) diameter circle. Alternatively, you may wish to roll out all the dough to a 1½ cm (½in) thickness and cut out 6 rounds of dough with a 12cm (4½in) pastry cutter. This will give a more uniform shape.
4. Place buns on a greased baking tray, cover with a clean towel and allow to rise for 20 minutes. Brush with milk, sprinkle with sesame seeds and bake in a preheated oven, 200°C (400°F) for 10 minutes then reduce heat to 180°C (350°F) and cook for a further 15 minutes or until they are golden and sound hollow when tapped.
5. Assemble the buns with a combination of burger, salad, cheese, pickles, fried egg and ketchup.

Hot Dog Buns

Preparation 40 mins **Cooking** 1 hr **Calories** 1936

280ml (10 fl oz) tepid water
1 tbsp margarine
1 x 60g (2oz) egg
500g (18oz) white bread mix
1½ tsps instant dry yeast

1 Place all ingredients into the bread pan in the order listed, insert into the breadmaker and close the lid.

2 Program: Dough Press: Start.

3 Turn completed dough onto a lightly floured suface. Divide dough into 6 or 8 pieces. Roll out each piece into a 10 or 13cm (4 or 5in) circle and almost 1cm (⅓ in) thick.

4 To shape the hot dog bun, fold the circle two-thirds of the way across the diameter, then fold remaining third over to meet opposite edge. Place seam side down on a greased baking tray. When all are completed, cover with a clean towel and set aside in a warm place to rise for 20 to 30 minutes.

5 Brush with milk, place in a preheated oven 200°C (400°F) for 10 minutes, and reduce heat. Cook for 10 minutes more until they are golden and sound hollow when tapped.

6 Assemble buns with grilled sausage or steamed frankfurt, mustard and pickles of your choice.

Index